The Official
QUEENS PARK
RANGERS
Annual 2009

Written By

Francis Aitkinson & Ian Taylor

g

A Grange Publication

© 2008. Published by Grange Communications Ltd., Edinburgh, under licence from Queens Park Rangers Football Club.

Printed in the EU.

Photographs © Action Images

ISBN 978-1-906211-57-8

£6.99

4

Contents

Bristol City 2, QPR 2

Damion Stewart's last-gasp equaliser gave Rangers a deserved share of the spoils at Ashton Gate. The Jamaican international defender pounced in the dying seconds, as Rangers came from behind twice to kick off their Championship campaign with a point. Moments earlier, Scott Murray appeared to have handed the Championship newcomers all three points, when he curled home a 90th minute stunner.

In truth, a point was the least the R's deserved, with the woodwork twice denying the outstanding Martin Rowlands in a second half dominated by the visitors. Man of the match Rowlands hit the post and the bar and had two stunning efforts saved by Stephen Henderson. Earlier, John Gregory's men came from behind to draw level at the break.

Lee Johnson cashed in on a poor defensive clearance from John Curtis to open the scoring on 32 minutes, but the lead lasted less than two minutes. Dexter Blackstock opened his account for the new campaign, when he nipped in behind a static Robins' rearguard and lobbed the advancing Adriano Basso.

QPR 1, Leyton Orient 2

Rangers bowed out of the Carling Cup to League One side Leyton Orient at a rain-swept Loftus Road. Two goals in a nine minute purple patch early in the second half gave Martin Ling's outfit the initiative, as the R's were left to rue a hatful of missed half-chances in the first period. Martin Rowlands provided brief hope with a quarter of the tie to go, but earlier strikes from Jason Demetriou and Adam Boyd (pen) ultimately proved to be enough for the O's to progress.

QPR 0, Cardiff City 2

Goals from Steven MacLean and Paul Parry gave Cardiff a 2-0 victory at Loftus Road, on a frustrating afternoon for the hosts.

The Bluebirds made the most of a below-par performance from the R's to leave W12 with maximum points. MacLean opened the scoring on 29 minutes, when he capitalised on hesitancy in the Rangers penalty area to smash the ball past Lee Camp from close range.

Rangers started the second period encouragingly, but just as it did seven days earlier, the woodwork thwarted their efforts. Stefan Moore's shot bounced back off the post, before Danny Nardiello was denied at point-blank range by Ross Turnbull. The all-important second Bluebirds goal arrived moments after Nardiello's chance, as Parry headed home from the edge of the six-yard box to all but clinch the result.

QPR 0, Southampton 3

Rangers slumped to a 3-0 defeat at the hands of Southampton, as the heartbreaking events of the last week took their toll on John Gregory's side. Ray Jones' untimely death seven days earlier was clearly still playing on the minds of the QPR players, as they succumbed to a second home league loss of the campaign. A first half brace from Grzegorz Rasiak and a second half header from Bradley Wright-Phillips put Rangers to the sword, in front of the watching Flavio Briatore.

Leicester City 1, QPR 1

Mikele Leigertwood bagged an early contender for goal of the season, as the R's came from behind to clinch a deserved point at the Walkers Stadium. With the clock showing 82 minutes, the former Sheffield United ace let fly from fully 28-yards, giving Foxes custodian Marton Fulop absolutely no chance as the ball nestled into the far corner. Earlier, Iain Hume's 63rd minute spot-kick looked like giving Leicester the points. The diminutive attacker made no mistake from the spot, after Damion Stewart was adjudged to have sent DJ Campbell spiralling to ground inside the box.

QPR 0, Plymouth Argyle 2

Second half goals from Peter Halmosi and David Norris heaped more misery on the R's at Loftus Road. The Hoops' winless streak in W12 extended to five matches, as Plymouth boss Ian Holloway guided his side to a memorable victory at his former stomping ground. Halmosi opened the scoring four minutes into the second half, before Norris put the result beyond any doubt with a close-range strike on 62 minutes.

QPR 1, Watford 1

Ten-man Rangers shared the spoils with table-toppers Watford in a pulsating local derby in W12. Substitute Stefan Moore's first goal since December 2005 proved decisive, as the R's came from behind to gain a morale-booting point against Aidy Boothroyd's high-flying outfit. Earlier, Middlesbrough loanee Adam Johnson put the Hornets in front in the 49th minute, when he headed home Tommy Smith's back post cross. Moore put Rangers on level terms though with a spectacular close range strike, and after Mikele Leigertwood saw red for two bookable offences, Rangers had strong appeals for a spot-kick waved away, when Dexter Blackstock appeared to be sent tumbling to ground by Lloyd Doyley.

West Bromwich Albion 5, QPR 1

Kevin Phillips bagged a brace, as free-scoring West Bromwich Albion produced a five-star show to extinguish the R's unbeaten away run. The R's trailed 3-1 at the end of an enthralling first period. Albion opened the scoring in the 18th minute courtesy of Phillips, before he turned provider for Ishmael Miller, who sprinted beyond a static Rangers rearguard to make it two 60 seconds later. The R's briefly rallied and when Gareth Ainsworth made it 2-1 when he smashed the ball home from close range in the 24th minute, the visitors sensed a revival. But Albion restored their two-goal buffer just before the break, as Phillips notched a sublime goal, curling the ball past Lee Camp from the edge of the penalty box. The rampant hosts made certain of the victory early in the second half, when Robert Koren smashed an unstoppable strike past Camp, before Jonathan Greening sent a fearsome 25-yard volley into the far corner to make it five.

Colchester United 4, QPR 2.

The R's succumbed to back-to-back defeats, as Colchester notched up their first home victory of the campaign at Layer Road. A debut goal from Rowan Vine and a first in QPR colours from Hogan Ephraim proved scant consolation for Rangers, who remain rooted to the foot of the Championship table. QPR trailed 3-1 at the end of a lively first period. After Lee Camp tipped Mark Yeates' initial effort onto the bar, Mikele Leigertwood's outstretched leg diverted the ball into the R's net to hand Colchester an 18th minute lead. The R's were level just 11 minutes later though, with Ephraim notching his first goal for the Club, when he pounced on Vine's sublime pass before slotting the ball under Dean Gerken. Rangers switched off immediately though, and the U's took full advantage. Kemal Izzet headed past the exposed Camp to make it 2-1, before Yeates made it three in the 38th minute, firing home - via a deflection - from a dubiously awarded free-kick. Vine gave Rangers hope when he finished with aplomb in the 58th minute for a thoroughly deserved debut goal, but the R's were their own worst enemies three minutes later, when Clive Platt stooped to head home the U's fourth.

QPR 1, Norwich City 0

Martin Rowlands' second half spot-kick ensured QPR headed into the international break on a high with a first victory of the campaign, in front of the live Sky Sports cameras. Rowlands bagged the only goal of a one-sided contest midway through the second period, when referee Peter Walton pointed to the spot following Ian Murray's foul on home debutant Rowan 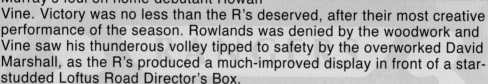 Vine. Victory was no less than the R's deserved, after their most creative performance of the season. Rowlands was denied by the woodwork and Vine saw his thunderous volley tipped to safety by the overworked David Marshall, as the R's produced a much-improved display in front of a star-studded Loftus Road Director's Box.

QPR 1, Ipswich Town 1

Second half substitute Marc Nygaard came off the bench to salvage a point for the R's against mid-table Ipswich Town. The Danish striker, returning after a two month lay-off with a calf injury, bagged his first goal of the season in the 72nd minute at a sun drenched Loftus Road. Earlier, Sylvan Legwinski put the Tractor Boys in front, when he smashed an unstoppable volley past Lee Camp from fully 22-yards. After Nygaard made it 1-1, Rangers went in search of a winner. Adam Bolder saw his vocal appeals for a spot-kick turned down, while the hardworking Rowan Vine pulled a volley inches wide of Neil Alexander's right hand post, as the R's finished on top.

Preston North End 0, QPR 0

Rangers stretched their unbeaten run to three games, with a plucky point at Deepdale. Lee Camp's first half spot-kick save proved decisive, as the R's battled heroically to clinch a point in Lancashire. The hosts left the field to a chorus of boos from their own supporters - clear evidence of a job well done by the visitors.

Charlton Athletic 0, QPR 1

Skipper Adam Bolder bagged his first goal for the Club as Rangers beat high-flying Charlton to clinch their first away win of the season. Bolder's 72nd minute strike capped an excellent second-half display as the R's shrugged off the setback of a penalty miss from Martin Rowlands.

QPR 2, Hull City 0

'Rangers are back' cheered the Loftus Road masses and after a performance like this, few could argue with the 12,000-plus crowd. Sensational strikes from Hogan Ephraim and Mikele Leigertwood lit up W12, to cap a perfect opening day for new First Team Coach Luigi De Canio. Ephraim opened the scoring in the 26th minute, cutting inside from his left wing position before firing an unstoppable 22-yard strike past Boaz Myhill. The R's continued to dominate and Leigertwood rubber-stamped the performance early in the second half, when he curled home only his second goal in QPR colours. The victory increased the R's unbeaten run to five matches in all competitions.

QPR 1, Coventry City 2

Kevin Kyle's last-gasp header clinched it for City, as the Sky Blues came from behind to register all three points at Loftus Road.
The second half substitute nodded the all-important third goal of the game in the first minute of stoppage time, to deny Rangers a share of the spoils. Earlier, Michael Mifsud cancelled out Akos Buzsaky's first goal in QPR colours. After Rangers lost three players to injury in a disrupted first period, the R's went in front early in the second half, courtesy of Buzsaky's 20-yard effort. Misfud restored parity with a well-taken goal on the hour, before Kyle's late heroics sent the travelling Sky Blues faithful home happy.

Crystal Palace 1, QPR 1

Rangers' nemesis Clinton Morrison denied them a deserved three points as he bagged his 100th Palace goal to cancel out Scott Sinclair's opener at Selhurst Park. Morrison has now netted five times in the last six meetings between the clubs - but the R's should have sewn up victory after squandering a host of chances in the second half.

QPR 0, Sheffield Wednesday 0

Quite how this match finished goalless will remain a mystery for a long time to come. Following on from the draw at Crystal Palace prior to the international break, Rangers yet again dominated a Championship fixture, but were left with only a point to show for their efforts. Missed chances, fantastic saves and the intervention of the woodwork on no less than four separate occasions turned a potential goal-fest into a stalemate.

Stoke City 3, QPR 1

A brave second half display from the visitors proved immaterial, as ten-man Rangers succumbed to a 3-1 defeat at The Britannia Stadium. In a first half dominated by the Potters, goals from Richard Cresswell (5) and Liam Lawrence (20) put the hosts firmly in the driving seat. Cresswell opened the scoring with a simple far post tap-in from a Rory Delap long throw-in, before Lawrence stunned the travelling R's faithful with a set-piece special from fully 20-yards after 20 minutes. Bad turned to worse for Rangers inside the opening two minutes of the second half, when Dexter Blackstock was shown a straight red card for a late tackle on Ryan Shawcross. And although Rowan Vine provided brief hope when he lashed a stunning strike past Steve Simonsen from range, Stoke soon restored their two-goal buffer when Leon Cort headed home the hosts third 14 minutes from time.

DECEMBER

Blackpool 1, QPR 0
Ben Burgess' 91st minute goal clinched it for Blackpool, on a disappointing afternoon for the R's. The Seasiders' front-man headed past the otherwise outstanding Lee Camp in the first minute of stoppage time, to send Rangers back to the Capital with nothing to show for their efforts. The R's, to their credit, worked tirelessly, but the swirling wind made it almost impossible for the visitors to play the expansive football the Rangers faithful have become accustomed to in recent weeks.

QPR 1, Crystal Palace 2
Two goals in two second half minutes from the visitors condemned Rangers to a 2-1 defeat in W12. Clint Hill and R's nemesis Clinton Morrison struck midway through the half, to send the Hoops to the foot of the Championship table. Earlier, Damion Stewart gave Rangers the initiative with his second goal of the campaign, heading home Akos Buzsaky's tenth minute corner. But in truth, Palace were good value for their victory in the second half, as Rangers' poor form continued.

Scunthorpe United 2, QPR 2
Akos Buzsaky's deadly double clinched Rangers a creditable point at Glanford Park. The midfield maestro bagged a brace of contenders for goal of the season, on an afternoon when the R's twice threw away a lead against fellow strugglers Scunthorpe United. Buzsaky's first half double saw Rangers into the break with a 2-1 lead, after Martin Paterson put the Iron on level terms midway through the first half. Iron's reward for an electrifying start to the second half arrived courtesy of Jonathan Forte's 54th minute strike and although both sides went in search of a winning goal, a draw was probably a fair reflection.

Burnley 0, QPR 2
Second half goals from Damion Stewart and Rowan Vine clinched a thoroughly deserved victory for Rangers against in-form Burnley at Turf Moor. Jamaican international defender Stewart opened the scoring on the hour with a precise downward header, before Vine capitalised on Gabor Kiraly's ill-fated decision to come forward for a late Burnley corner, netting his third goal of the season in style. Victory was no less than the R's deserved, on a night when their committed performance provided a fitting send-off to former team-mate Ray Jones, who passed away hours before this fixture was originally scheduled to take place back in the opening month of the season.

QPR 0, Wolverhampton Wanderers 0
A goalkeeping master-class from Wayne Hennessey prevented Rangers from rounding off a near-perfect week with victory at Loftus Road. The Wolves custodian ultimately proved to be the difference in W12, on an afternoon when the R's again showed signs of a return to form following a poor run of results that had seen them slip to the foot of the Championship. Hennessey - the Welsh international goalkeeper - twice denied R's skipper Martin Rowlands, while strong appeals for a second half penalty, when Marc Nygaard was dragged to ground, fell on deaf ears.

QPR 2, Colchester United 1
Akos Buzsaky enhanced his ever-growing reputation with two sublime individual goals, as ten-man Rangers sealed a crucial home victory

against fellow strugglers Colchester United. The Hungarian international capped a cameo individual display with a goal in each half, to lift the R's off the foot of the Championship table. Mark Yeates ensured a nervy finale when he pulled a goal back in the 62nd minute, but - despite Damion Stewart seeing red for two bookable offences late on - Rangers held on for three priceless points.

Plymouth Argyle 2, QPR 1
The Rangers revival faltered on Boxing Day, as Luigi De Canio's men fought hard, but conceded a late, late goal to lose 2-1 at Plymouth. The R's took the lead at Home Park on 19 minutes when Rowan Vine slotted home at the far post following good work by Akos Buzsaky and Martin Rowlands. But right at the start of the second half Argyle drew level with a Sylvan Ebanks-Blake spot-kick after Simon Walton was adjudged to have handled in the box. And the R's had to swallow a bitter pill of defeat when Ebanks-Blake netted in the fourth minute of injury time following a Peter Halmosi corner. The visitors were left devastated at the final whistle after fighting so hard but, in the end, having nothing to show for their efforts.

Watford 2, QPR 4
Rangers ran riot at Vicarage Road, as goals from Martin Rowlands (2), Damion Stewart and Akos Buzsaky clinched a stunning 4-2 victory against Championship front-runners Watford. The R's stormed into a three goal lead at the break. Rowlands opened the scoring from the spot, before he turned provider to set up Stewart who headed home to make it two. The outstanding Rowlands capped a cameo individual display with a third from Angelo Balanta's threaded through ball, and although a Lee Camp own goal temporarily allowed the Hornets back into the tie early in the second period, substitute Akos Buzsaky guaranteed the win eight minutes from time. Remarkably, there was still time for R's old-boy Danny Shittu to notch a late second for the Hornets, but it was Rangers' day - and how!

JANUARY

QPR 3, Leicester City 1
The R's revival continued on New Year's Day, as fellow strugglers Leicester City were put to the sword at a raucous Loftus Road.
In a one-sided first half, Damion Stewart opened the scoring with his fourth goal in seven outings, before Adam Bolder made it 2-0 with a close range header. Dexter Blackstock all but guaranteed maximum points for the hosts when he soared to head home number three, and although Iain Hume pulled a goal back with a spectacular free-kick, the R's made it nine points out of 12 over the festive period - and in some style too. Vengeance!

Chelsea 1, QPR 0
QPR left Stamford Bridge with their heads held high, despite bowing out of the FA Cup to holders and near-neighbours Chelsea. A fluke goal in the 29th minute proved to be the difference between the West London rivals, on an afternoon when the R's impressive performance promised much for a very bright future. Lee Camp was the unlucky culprit, as Claudio Pizarro's right foot shot bounced back off the post and hit the unfortunate keeper, before trickling over the line. Despite the final scoreline, Rangers were by no means overawed by their hosts, with Martin Rowlands and Gavin Mahon at the heart of their efficient display.

Sheffield United 2, QPR 1
Rangers surrendered a one goal lead, as Sheffield United came from behind to clinch a 2-1 victory at Bramall Lane. The R's appeared to be on

their way to maximum points when Patrick Agyemang opened the scoring on the stroke of half-time, but a Damion Stewart own goal and Lee Hendrie's first league goal of the campaign sealed it for the Blades. Defeat was harsh on Rangers, who did more than enough to warrant a point, on an afternoon when two fortuitous goals proved to be their undoing.

QPR 2, Barnsley 0
New-boys Patrick Agyemang and Rowan Vine were on target, as Rangers eased to a comfortable 2-0 victory against out-of-sorts Barnsley. In front of the biggest crowd of the campaign, the R's were good value for the two goal win, which extended their unbeaten home run to four matches. In a first half which largely flattered to deceive, Rangers were perhaps a little fortunate to head into the break with a two-goal buffer. Agyemang opened the scoring inside the opening five minutes with a tidy finish, before Vine made it two on the stroke of half-time, after the former Preston man played provider.

Cardiff City 3, QPR 1
In-form Cardiff City continued their march to the top-six with a domineering display against out-of-sorts Rangers. In a first period totally dominated by the hosts, Joe Ledley opened the scoring in the 13th minute, before the midfield maestro doubled the Bluebirds' advantage four minutes before the break. There was nothing the outstanding Lee Camp could do to prevent Paul Parry making it three early in the second half, as the forward coasted through unmarked to notch the Bluebirds' third. To their credit, Rangers continued to plug away as the clock ticked down, and they were rewarded when Patrick Agyemang fired home his third in as many games after Michael Oakes dropped Hogan Ephraim's cross under pressure from Dexter Blackstock.

FEBRUARY

QPR 3, Bristol City 0
Rangers bounced back in emphatic fashion against high-flying Bristol City, as Patrick Agyemang's scintillating form continued with a deadly double. The former Preston North End front-man - currently enjoying the richest goalscoring form of his career - bagged a first half brace, before Akos Buzsaky put the icing on the cake for the hosts with yet another stunning contender for goal of the season. The 3-0 victory - Rangers' fourth win in a row at Loftus Road - put the ghost of the R's display at Ninian Park firmly to rest, as Championship front-runners Bristol City were out-classed and out-fought in every department.

Southampton 2, QPR 3
History repeated itself at St Mary's, as Rangers came back from a goal down to clinch all three points against managerless Southampton. Following last season's comeback victory on the South Coast, the R's again left the home faithful stunned, as a brace from Patrick Agyemang and a sublime Martin Rowlands goal wiped out Darren Powell's first minute strike. The victory - Rangers' first on their travels since the turn of the year - again owed much to Agyemang, who enhanced his ever-glowing reputation with a deadly double; his second of the season against

the Saints, following his two goal salvo in early October for former club Preston North End. To compound the hosts' woes, skipper Youssef Safri was shown a straight red card in the closing stages for a reckless challenge on Agyemang and although Stern John bagged a late second for the hosts, it was Rangers' day - and deservedly so.

QPR 2, Burnley 4

Former England striker Andy Cole rolled back the years with a hat-trick, as Rangers tasted defeat at Loftus Road for the first time in 2008. Trailing 2-0 inside the opening half hour, Owen Coyle's men came back from the dead to win 4-2, in an extraordinary Championship encounter. Gavin Mahon's first goal in 10 months put Rangers in front early on and when Patrick Agyemang made it two in the 30th minute, the R's faithful sensed another comfortable home win. But Burnley had other ideas and thanks to Cole's deadly treble and a close range header from Ade Akinbiyi, the Clarets exacted revenge for the R's 2-0 win at Turf Moor in December - and in some style too.

QPR 1, Sheffield United 1

Honours ended even in West London, as Chris Morgan's late leveller denied the R's maximum points in an eagerly-contested mid-table battle. Only goal difference separated the two Clubs at the start of the day, but with Rangers enjoying the lion's share of territory and possession throughout the 90 minutes, Luigi De Canio's men will look back at what might have been after Angelo Balanta's early goal put them in the driving seat. The youngster's first senior goal on his full debut was the R's just reward for a positive first half showing, yet despite Martin Rowlands and Rowan Vine each going close to doubling the hosts' advantage, United weathered the storm and they were rewarded when Morgan rifled home his second of the season late on.

Barnsley 0, QPR 0

Rangers ground out a plucky point against home specialists Barnsley, on a night when skill and style had to make way for passion and determination at a wind-swept Oakwell. Neither side did enough to warrant maximum points, as both Clubs remained deadlocked on 41 points in the Championship table. Skipper Martin Rowlands did his best to haul Rangers to victory, but the all-important breakthrough goal failed to materialise.

13

QPR 3, Stoke 0

Mikele Leigertwood doubled his goals tally for the season with a brilliant brace, as Rangers ran riot against 10-man Stoke City in front of the live Sky Sports cameras. Two-goal hero Leigertwood was joined on the scoresheet by Akos Buzsaky, on a day when Luigi De Canio's men totally out-foxed Tony Pulis' Championship front-runners. To compound the visitors' woes, skipper Andy Griffin was harshly sent off in the 42nd minute, for a mistimed lunge on the influential Hogan Ephraim. In truth, the margin of victory flattered Stoke, who were grateful to goalkeeper Steve Simonsen for keeping the scoreline down.

Coventry City 0, QPR 0

Lee Camp was in inspirational form, as Rangers extended their mini unbeaten run to four Championship matches with a creditable point against Coventry City. The R's number one was unbeatable at The Ricoh Arena, as the visitor's battled their way to a valuable draw. In a one-sided first half, Camp saved twice from Leon Best and once from Jay Tabb, as Chris Coleman's side orchestrated proceedings. Rangers, to their credit, improved after the break, and went closest to breaking the deadlock, when Akos Buzsaky fired onto the roof of the net.

Sheffield Wednesday 2, QPR 1

The Owls' hoodoo sign over QPR continued, as Brian Laws' men came from behind to clinch a crucial victory in their quest to pull away from the Championship drop-zone. The 2-1 defeat, which leaves the R's just six clear of safety, means Rangers have now failed to beat Sheffield Wednesday, home or away, since our promotion party at Hillsborough four years ago. Damien Delaney gave Luigi De Canio's men a dream start with his first goal in QPR colours in the 15th minute, only for Wednesday to hit back on the stroke of half-time courtesy of Graham Kavanagh. And when Lee Camp was penalised for sending Sean McAllister to ground six minutes into the second half, substitute Deon Burton made no mistake from the spot to complete an unlikely turnaround. Hogan Ephraim saw red late on for raising his arms in the direction of Franck Songo'o, as the R's day went from bad to worse.

QPR 3, Blackpool 2

The race for the golden boot stepped up a notch, as Akos Buzsaky, Rowan Vine and Martin Rowlands were each on target in the R's 3-2 victory against Blackpool. In the presence of the Club's three major investors - Flavio Briatore, Bernie Ecclestone and Lakshmi Mittal - as well as the King of Ghana and Real Madrid president Ramon Calderon, Buzsaky's ninth of the season set the tone, before Vine made it two with a fine drilled effort - his sixth of the campaign - in the 35th minute. Rowlands slammed home his sixth of the season to make it 3-0 early in the second half, and although Ben Burgess (61) and Stephen McPhee (73) set up a grandstand finish, Rangers held on and propelled themselves into the top half of the table for the first time this season.

QPR 3, Scunthorpe United 1

Martin Rowlands, Patrick Agyemang and Rowan Vine were all on target, as the R's came from behind to send Scunthorpe United spiralling towards League One. Rangers trailed to Grant McCann's fine free-kick, only for the hosts to respond courtesy of a debatable Rowlands spot-kick. Agyemang put the R's in front when he smashed home Akos Buzsaky's classy 79th minute through ball, before Vine put the icing on the cake with a well-taken third goal in stoppage time.

Wolverhampton Wanderers 3, QPR 3

Wolves scored a 95th minute equaliser in a thrilling 3-3 draw at Molineux this afternoon, although the R's will be desperately disappointed not to have won, having led on three separate occasions. In bizarre weather conditions which included sun, rain and snow, Akos Buzsaky had earlier given Luigi De Canio's men the lead before Andy Keogh drew matters level just before the break. Early in the second half, Rangers were awarded a spot-kick when Neill Collins handled inside the area. Dexter Blackstock made no mistake, but Wolves were soon level when referee Clive Oliver awarded his second penalty of the afternoon for a foul by 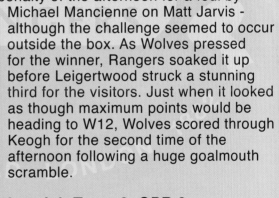 Michael Mancienne on Matt Jarvis - although the challenge seemed to occur outside the box. As Wolves pressed for the winner, Rangers soaked it up before Leigertwood struck a stunning third for the visitors. Just when it looked as though maximum points would be heading to W12, Wolves scored through Keogh for the second time of the afternoon following a huge goalmouth scramble.

Ipswich Town 0, QPR 0

In a fixture between two of the Championship's great entertainers, Ipswich and QPR fought out a compelling stalemate at Portman Road. Danny Haynes hit the post for the Tractor Boys in the first-half, while Hogan Ephraim blasted wide with the goal at his mercy, as the R's more than matched Jim Magilton's men in every department. Rangers upped the tempo after the break and in the end, were good value for their point.

QPR 2, Preston North End 2

Gareth Ainsworth came off the bench to inspire Rangers to an unlikely share of the spoils against Preston North End. The R's midfielder scored one and made another, as Luigi De Canio's men staged a late salvo at Loftus Road. Trailing to Neil Mellor's first half strike and a Matthew Connolly own goal, Ainsworth fired an unstoppable half-volley past Andy Lonergan in the 90th minute, before Dexter Blackstock soared to head home an equaliser in the third minute of added time.

Hull City 1, QPR 1

An injury-time equaliser denied Rangers their first league double of the season as Hull snatched a point at the KC Stadium. Dexter Blackstock was credited with the controversial 13th-minute strike that gave the R's a lead they held for almost the entire game, but Michael Turner rescued the promotion hopefuls in stoppage time.

QPR 1, Charlton Athletic 0

Dexter Blackstock continued his rich vein of form with the only goal of the game, as the R's completed their first double of the season in front of a season's high Loftus Road crowd of 17, 035. The R's front-man notched his fourth goal in five matches, to consign the Addicks to yet another season in the Coca Cola Championship. Rangers - inspired by the excellent Martin Rowlands - were dominant throughout, with Lee Camp a virtual spectator in the R's goal, as Charlton failed to muster a single noteworthy effort on goal throughout the 90 minutes.

Norwich City 3, QPR 0

An inexplicable refereeing decision inside the opening five minutes cost Rangers dear at Carrow Road, as the R's slumped to their first defeat in eight Championship fixtures. Damion Stewart was harshly given his marching orders in the fifth minute - and in truth, the R's never really recovered. Ched Evans opened the scoring moments after the referee's surprise decision and when Mark Fotheringham's deflected effort made it two early in the second half, the R's were soon facing up to their sixth straight defeat at Carrow Road. Canaries substitute Darel Russell put the icing on the cake for Norwich eight minutes from time, firing home from distance after Lee Camp was dispossessed whilst attempting to clear his lines.

QPR 0, West Bromwich Albion 2

Martin Rowlands saw red, as the Baggies bounced back to the top tier of English football as Champions of the Coca Cola Championship. The R's midfielder was the unfortunate recipient of one of the more harsher sending-offs of the campaign, when he was given his marching orders just before half-time for a mistimed tackle on Jonathan Greening. Albion's numerical advantage told after the break, when Kim Do-Hoen nodded Tony Mowbray's men in front, before Chris Brunt put the icing on the cake for the Midlands outfit with a late second. In truth, the final scoreline was harsh on the R's, who competed valiantly with ten men, with Gareth Ainsworth at the heart of everything positive for the hosts in front of a season's high crowd of 18, 309.

When Martin Rowlands hit double figures for only the second time in his career during the 2006/07 season, many R's supporters probably thought they'd seen the very best of the midfield maestro. The Hammersmith born midfielder had other ideas though and duly went on to scale even greater heights last season.

From his opening day display against Bristol City at Ashton Gate, you kind of sensed this was going to be a season to remember for the former Brentford man. Rowlands was instrumental in the 2-2 draw against Gary Johnson's Championship newcomers, and but for the intervention of the woodwork, on another day would have returned to West London with the matchball in his hand.

As his fine start to the season continued, unsurprisingly it was Rowlands who bagged the all-important winner against Norwich City in October, as Rangers chalked up a much needed opening victory of the campaign.

But arguably his finest hour of another memorable season arrived at Vicarage Road – the home of local rivals Watford – in the final fixture of 2007.

Having opened the scoring from the penalty spot, Rowlands then turned provider for Damion Stewart to double the R's early advantage. The outstanding Rowlands capped a cameo individual display with a third from Angelo Balanta's threaded through ball, and although a Lee Camp own goal temporarily allowed the Hornets back into the tie early in the second period, substitute Akos Buzsaky guaranteed the win eight minutes from time. Remarkably, there was still time for R's old-boy Danny Shittu to notch a late second for the Hornets, but it was Rangers' day – and Rowland's was at the heart of it all.

Six goals and three assists from centre midfield again represented a decent return for the R's skipper, and with Giovanni Trapattoni acknowledging his displays with a call-up to his first Eire squad at the end of the campaign, it appears Rowlands is destined for even greater things next season.

PLAYER OF THE YEAR - MARTIN ROWLANDS

YOUNG PLAYER OF THE YEAR - MICHAEL MANCIENNE

After finishing runner-up to Dexter Blackstock 12 months earlier, Michael Mancienne went one better last season by scooping the prestigious Young Player of the Year crown.

The Chelsea loanee, who is regarded as one of the brightest young prospects within the English game, made 31 appearances in all competitions for the R's and rarely put a foot wrong.

Equally adept with the ball at his feet or in the air, Mancienne shone at right back for the majority of the campaign and when asked to do so, filled in at centre back in similarly efficient fashion.

Chants of 'sign him up, sign him up, sign him up' were regularly heard reverberating around the Loftus Road terraces and although Mancienne himself readily admits to not knowing where his long term future lies, it's safe to say, he's destined to go on and achieve great things in the game.

GOAL OF THE SEASON

It was a goal fit to grace any stadium in the world.

When Patrick Agyemang's cross landed at the feet of Akos Buzsaky, no-one in the 11,000-plus crowd could have possibly envisaged what would happen next.

With his back to goal, the Magical Magyar cleverly adjusted his body before craftily lofting a deft, half-volleyed chip beyond the stranded Paul Rachubka and in off the underside of the bar.

You couldn't help but feel sorry for Rachubka, who stood motionless as the ball ballooned beyond him and in to the back of the net. For Buzsaky, the goal only served to enhance his ever-growing reputation in W12.

The midfielder scored a remarkable ten goals in just 28 appearances, but this was the pick – and rightly so.

Rangers ran out worthy 3-2 winners on the night, picking up a valuable three points which rocketed them into the top half of the table for the first time. In the presence of the Club's three major investors - Flavio Briatore, Bernie Ecclestone and Lakshmi Mittal - as well as the King of Ghana and Real Madrid president Ramon Calderon, Buzsaky's ninth of the season set the tone, before Rowan Vine made it two with a fine drilled effort - his sixth of the campaign - in the 35th minute.

Rowlands slammed home his sixth of the season to make it 3-0 early in the second half, and although Ben Burgess (61) and Stephen McPhee (73) set up a grandstand finish, Rangers held on and Buzsaky walked off with his name up in lights.

THE GOAL-DEN BOY

AKOS BUZSAKY
QPR 3 - Blackpool 2
Tuesday 11th March 2008

Luigi De Canio: In Profile

After a ten year playing career in the Italian lower leagues, Luigi De Canio started his coaching career in the late nineties with Pisticci, who he guided to Serie D. He spent four more seasons with the Club, before joining Serie C outfit Savoia during the 1993/94 campaign. De Canio enjoyed a successful start to life at his new Club, leading them to promotion, albeit via the play-off's, in his first season in charge.

A switch to Serie C1 side Siena followed in 1995/96, with De Canio achieving an eighth place finish in his first season in charge of the Robur. Short stints at Carpi and Lucchese followed, before De Canio showed his undoubted managerial credentials at Pescara. He led the Club to the brink of promotion to Serie A, which led to interest from a number of top-flight Clubs in the Italian league, including Udinese, who secured his services in 1999/2000.

De Canio adjusted to life in the top-flight accordingly, guiding the Biaconeri to an eighth place finish and a place in the UEFA Intertoto Cup. UEFA Cup football duly followed after a successful Intertoto campaign, but despite an encouraging start to the new season, a dreadful run of form, which culminated with a home defeat to Parma, resulted in his departure in March 2001.

Napoli swooped to secure his services in 2001/02, but a fifth place finish in Serie B was deemed a failure and De Canio consequently parted company with the Azzurri. Serie A Club Reggina was his next port of call, before De Canio replaced the legendary Roberto Donadoni at the helm of Serie B side Genoa. Despite staving off the ever-looming threat of relegation with a 16th place finish, De Canio was sacked on the eve of the 2004/05 campaign.

He spent six months out of the game before re-joining Siena, whom he managed a decade earlier. Fourteenth and seventeenth placed finishes followed, prior to the appointment of Mario Beretta for the start of the 2006/07 season.

Mick Harford: In Profile

After a successful 21 year spell as a player, Mick Harford learned his managerial trade at former Club Wimbledon. It was there that he developed his skills, before following his old boss Joe Kinnear, back to Luton Town following Luton's relegation to Division Three. Harford helped master-mind the successful promotion season of 2001/02, as Luton stormed to promotion back to the Second Division. However, a takeover at the Bedfordshire-based outfit eventually saw him replaced, although Harford soon returned as Director of Football, as well as being first team coach, working alongside Mike Newell.

Harford helped Newell's Luton side to a tenth place finish and with his profile rising, he swapped a League One title quest with the Hatters, for a Championship dog-fight at Nottingham Forest, working as assistant to Kinnear. Kinnear was to last only a few more weeks at the Club, before Forest's poor form forced him to leave the City Ground. Harford was then appointed Caretaker Manager, and he performed admirably despite the problems at the Club. Gary Megson was then appointed Manager full time in January 2005, and Harford left the Club. Out of work for only a little while, Harford teamed up with Andy King at Swindon Town in a deal that would run until the end of the 2004/05 season. However, Harford never made it until the end of the season with Swindon, as in April 2005, he was appointed the new Manager of Rotherham United, who were relegated from the Championship at the end of the 2004/05 season.

Harford had an impressive start to his managerial career, but after a run of 17 games without a win, he was replaced by Alan Knill. Harford finished the season at Millwall, coaching the strikers at the Club before their relegation from the Championship at the end of the 2005/06 season. Harford then joined his former Derby County team-mate Geraint Williams at Colchester United in the summer of 2006, becoming the Club's Assistant Manager.

John Gregory: In Profile

John Gregory served his managerial apprenticeship at a variety of clubs. He started his career with Portsmouth, before a brief spell at Plymouth Argyle. Soon after he joined Leicester City in a coaching capacity, before being appointed First Team Coach at Villa Park in November 1994. He left Villa to become Manager of Wycombe Wanderers in October 1996.

After taking over a struggling Wanderers squad, he steered them clear of relegation in the 1996/97 season by eight points. He led Villa to the top of the Premiership following an unbeaten start to the season in 1998, which lasted a club record 12 matches. However, they were not able to sustain their title tilt and fell away in the second half of the season. In his four years in charge at Villa Park, the Villains never finished outside the top eight, finishing seventh in his first half-season as Manager, sixth in 1999 and 2000 and eighth in 2001.

Noted for speaking his mind, Gregory had his fair share of run-in's with players and Chairman Doug Ellis alike, but he was always 100 per cent committed to the Club and was unfortunate not to taste success in the FA Cup Final in 2000, losing to a single goal from Chelsea's Roberto di Matteo. He had criticised the club for failing to invest sufficiently in new players, but his passion and determination to lead Villa to glory remained undiminished. His departure came as a shock to players and fans alike and his achievements at Villa Park will be long-remembered by everyone connected with the Midlands Club.

He was immediately linked with the managerial vacancy at his old Club Derby County and, after being contacted by the Club about the position, he was unveiled as Colin Todd's successor on January 30 2002. His first priority at Pride Park was to keep The Rams in the Premiership, but with Derby lying second from bottom and six points adrift from safety at the time of his arrival, he was unable to save them. Despite a slight improvement in their results, The Rams were relegated to the First Division, and Gregory eventually left the Club in March 2003.

As a player, Gregory enjoyed a distinguished career, which saw him play for several teams. He was signed from apprentice at Northampton Town before moving to Aston Villa in 1977, where he spent two years before signing for Brighton. From there he went to QPR, in 1981, making 188 appearances for the R's, before signing for Derby County in 1985, staying with the Rams for two years before effectively hanging up his boots. Gregory was a tireless midfielder who made nearly 600 appearances in his career, scoring 83 goals, and winning six full international caps for England.

1. Lee CAMP
Goalkeeper (22-08-84)

After putting pen to paper on a £300,000 transfer from Derby County in the summer of 2007, Lee Camp was an ever-present in goal for the R's last season. The former England Under-21 stopper made 46 appearances in the Championship, keeping an impressive 14 clean sheets. His form was such that he was named runner-up in the Players' Player and Supporters' Player of the Year categories at the end of the season.

2. Damien DELANEY
Defender (20-07-81)

Damien Delaney penned a three-and-a-half year deal with Queens Park Rangers in January 2008. The left back was an instant hit amongst the R's faithful and opened his goalscoring account for his new Club against Sheffield Wednesday at Hillsborough in March. Delaney's form impressed new Republic of Ireland boss Giovanni Trapattoni too, with the defender making his full international debut in the summer international against Serbia in May.

3. Chris BARKER
Defender (02-03-80)

QPR secured the free transfer signing of Chris Barker in the summer of 2007, after the defender was released by Cardiff City. Barker, who spent the previous season on loan at Championship newcomers Colchester United, made 25 appearances in all competitions, despite undergoing two hernia operations.

4. Gavin MAHON
Midfielder (02-01-77)

Midfielder Gavin Mahon joined QPR in January 2008, making his debut from the substitutes' bench against Leicester City on New Years Day. A solid and reliable midfield general, Mahon - who skippered former club Watford to the Premiership during a five-year spell at Vicarage Road - opened his goalscoring account for the R's in the 4-2 defeat against Burnley.

5. Damion STEWART
Defender (18-08-80)

Jamaican international Damion Stewart signed a three-year contract with the R's in the summer of 2006. After a steady, if unspectacular start, Stewart was a virtual ever-present in his first campaign in W12 and then went on to enjoy a productive second season at Loftus Road. Stewart - who has amassed 30-plus appearances for his country and is nicknamed 'Stew Peas' by the Reggae Boyz - scored an impressive five goals from the back last season.

7. Adam BOLDER
Midfielder (25-10-80)

QPR signed Adam Bolder on a free transfer from Derby County on January 27th 2007. The no-nonsense midfielder penned a two and a half year deal at Loftus Road and in doing so, linked up with former Derby boss John Gregory. Bolder's impact was immediate in W12, as he galvanised a Rangers side heading in the wrong direction with a series of bustling displays in the heart of the R's midfield engine room. Bolder was appointed Club Captain at the start of the 2007/08 season, but went on to make just 13 appearances, before spending time on loan at Sheffield Wednesday.

8. Danny NARDIELLO
Striker (22-10-82)

QPR clinched the free transfer signing of Danny Nardiello in the summer of 2007. The former Manchester United ace agreed a two-year deal in W12, despite late interest from Championship rivals Norwich City. The Welsh international endured a frustrating maiden season in West London though, making just a handful of starts for the R's before returning to former club Barnsley on loan.

9. Dexter BLACKSTOCK
Striker (20-05-86)

QPR added to their attacking options by completing the signing of Southampton striker Dexter Blackstock, for an undisclosed fee, in August 2006. The hardworking front-man bagged 14 goals in all competitions in his maiden season at the Club and was deservedly named Young Player of the Year. Despite scoring on the opening day of the 2007/08 campaign, the England Under-21 international managed just six goals in all competitions last season - including four in the final seven matches of the season.

10. Akos BUZSAKY
Midfielder (07-05-82)

A player with outstanding individual ability, Akos Buzsaky made an immediate impact following his move to W12 from fellow Championship outfit Plymouth Argyle. The Hungarian international, who initially joined on loan prior to making the deal permanent in January 2008, scored six goals in his first 13 appearances, and ended the campaign with ten goals to his name. Buzsaky's taste for the spectacular also saw him scoop the Kiyan Prince Goal of the Season award, for a quite sublime effort against Blackpool in mid-March.

11. Gareth AINSWORTH
Midfielder (10-05-73)

Fans' favourite Gareth Ainsworth joined QPR after being released from Cardiff City in June 2003. The bustling midfielder's contribution to the Rangers cause has been without question ever since, providing leadership and guile, as well as priceless assists and match-winning goals. Despite two serious injuries during the 2006/07 campaign, Ainsworth returned stronger than ever last season, making 25 appearances in all competitions. After a brief stint assisting former Manager Luigi De Canio, the experienced midfielder was handed a player / coach role by Iain Dowie in the summer of 2008.

12. Jake COLE
Goalkeeper (11-05-85)

Jake Cole signed an improved contract until the summer of 2008 just days before the end of the 2005/06 season. The young goalkeeper made five appearances in all competitions in season 2006/07, but failed to make a single appearance last season.

14. Martin ROWLANDS
Midfielder (08-02-79)

Hammersmith-born midfielder Martin Rowlands joined Rangers in July 2003 on a free transfer from local rivals Brentford. The attacking midfielder hit double figures for only the second time in his career during the 2006/07 season, and followed it up with a series of virtuoso performances last season. As Rangers struggled early on in the wake of Ray Jones' untimely death, Rowlands rallied round his team-mates, scoring crucial goals against Norwich City, Watford and Southampton to name but a few. His reward came in the shape of an end-of-season awards double, Players' Player and Supporters' Player of the Year. After a four-year absence from the international fold, Rowlands was recalled to the full Republic of Ireland squad under new Eire boss Giovanni Trapattoni in April.

16. Matthew CONNOLLY
Defender (24-09-87)

Matthew Connolly penned a three-and-a-half year deal with the R's in January 2008. A product of the successful Arsenal academy, Connolly - who spent the first part of the 2007/08 season on loan at Championship rivals Colchester United - went on to make 21 appearances in all competitions for Rangers. After impressing during his first season in W12, Connolly received his first call up to Stuart Pearce's England Under-21 squad.

17. Patrick AGYEMANG
Striker (29-09-80)

Patrick Agyemang joined QPR from Preston in January 2008 on a four-and-a-half year deal, after the two Clubs agreed an undisclosed fee for his services. The Ghanaian international enjoyed a honeymoon period to remember for the R's, bagging eight goals in his first six league appearances. Agyemang went on to score nine goals in all competitions, as the R's climbed towards a comfortable mid-table position.

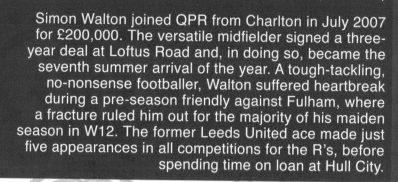

19. Simon WALTON
Midfielder (13-09-87)

Simon Walton joined QPR from Charlton in July 2007 for £200,000. The versatile midfielder signed a three-year deal at Loftus Road and, in doing so, became the seventh summer arrival of the year. A tough-tackling, no-nonsense footballer, Walton suffered heartbreak during a pre-season friendly against Fulham, where a fracture ruled him out for the majority of his maiden season in W12. The former Leeds United ace made just five appearances in all competitions for the R's, before spending time on loan at Hull City.

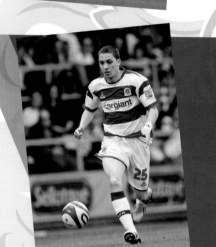

25. Hogan EPHRAIM
Midfielder (31-03-88)

After a successful loan spell in W12, winger Hogan Ephraim signed a three-and-a-half year contract with QPR in January 2008. The diminutive winger, who is considered one of the countries brightest prospects, is a graduate of the successful West Ham United academy. Ephraim made 30 appearances in all competitions last term, scoring two goals.

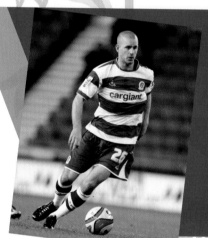

26. Rowan VINE
Striker (21-09-82)

Queens Park Rangers completed the signing of Birmingham City front-man Rowan Vine in January 2008. The experienced front-man signed a four-and-a-half year contract, after a successful loan period in W12. Vine went on to bag three crucial goals in 15 appearances during his first season at Loftus Road, prior to sustaining a fractured leg during a freak training ground accident in early April.

28. Zesh REHMAN
Defender (14-10-83)

QPR completed the signing of Fulham defender Zesh Rehman for an undisclosed fee in August 2006. The centre-half put pen to paper on a three year deal at Loftus Road, but it proved to be a maiden season to forget to the Pakistan centre-half. After a steady, if unspectacular, start at the heart of the Rangers' defence, Rehman found himself surplus to requirements under the guidance of John Gregory and was allowed to leave on loan in March 2007, linking up with former Club Brighton & Hove Albion. Rehman improved dramatically though last season, featuring on no fewer than 22 occasions for the R's.

29. Fitz HALL
Defender (20-12-80)

Fitz Hall penned a four-and-a-half year deal with Rangers at the start of the 2008 January transfer window, and made his debut in the FA Cup third round defeat at Chelsea. The defender, who gained vast Premiership experience during spells at Wigan Athletic and Crystal Palace, made 15 appearances in all competitions for the R's last season.

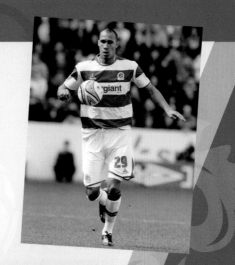

32. Mikele LEIGERTWOOD
Midfielder (12-11-82)

Rangers completed the signing of no-nonsense midfielder Mikele Leigertwood on the final day of the 2007 summer transfer window. The Sheffield United ace put pen to paper on a three-year deal, after the two Clubs agreed an undisclosed fee for his services. Leigertwood went on to play a crucial role during his first season at Loftus Road, scoring a creditable five goals in 40 league appearances.

36. Angelo BALANTA
Forward (01-07-90)

Teenage striker Angelo Balanta put pen-to-paper on his first professional contract with Queens Park Rangers Football Club in January 2008. The teenage Colombian, who made three First Team appearances in his time as an Under-18 player, inked a deal that keeps him at the Club until the summer of 2010. Balanta opened his goalscoring account for the R's with a classy close-range strike against Sheffield United in February 2008.

ANGELO BALANTA

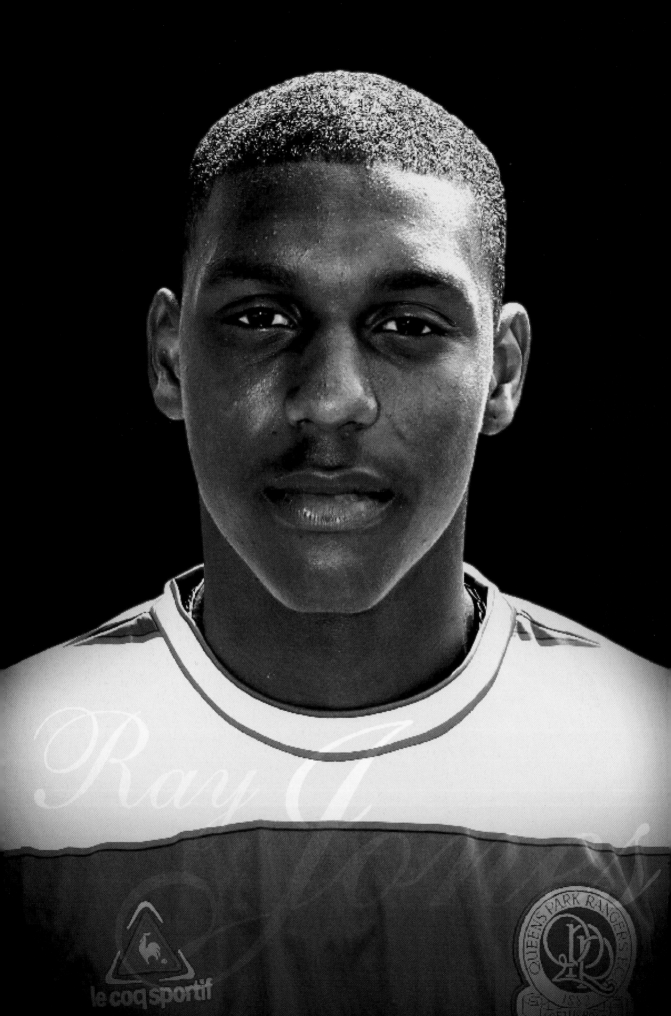

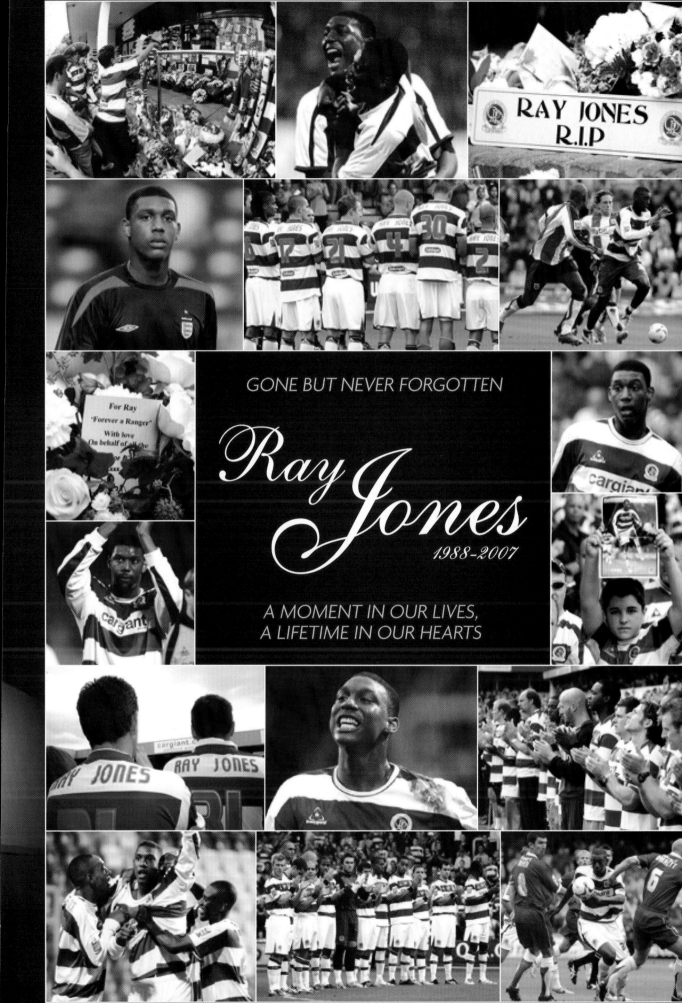

GONE BUT NEVER FORGOTTEN

Ray Jones

1988–2007

A MOMENT IN OUR LIVES,
A LIFETIME IN OUR HEARTS

SHOW YOUR
COLOURS

BUY NOW!

34

The BIG QPR Quiz

1. Who scored our first goal of the season on the opening day against Bristol City?

2. Which League One side knocked QPR out of the Carling Cup?

3. Which on-loan striker scored on his debut in the 4-2 defeat to Colchester United?

4. Which player scored the consolation goal in our 5-1 defeat to West Bromwich Albion?

5. Against which side did Rangers record their first victory of the season?

6. Who scored the only goal of the game in that win?

7. Which midfielder was sent off during the second half of the R's Boxing Day defeat at Plymouth?

8. Of the five matches Mick Harford was in charge, how many points did Rangers register?

9. Which player scored the first goal of Luigi De Canio's reign?

10. Which Chelsea loanee scored against Crystal Palace in the 1-1 draw at Selhurst Park?

11. Which player received his marching orders in the 3-1 defeat against Stoke City?

12. Which player scored twice in the 2-2 draw against Scunthorpe United?

13. Which member of the R's backroom staff did Damion Stewart run 70 yards to celebrate with following his goal against Burnley?

14. Which of their former team-mates did the R's dedicate that victory to?

15. Which Midlands side did Rangers share a goalless draw against in mid-November?

36

16. Which midfielder scored his first goal of the season in our 1-0 win at Charlton Athletic?

17. What was the half-time score when the R's won at Watford in the final match of 2007?

18. Which former Rangers defender scored for the Hornets in that match?

19. Who did Rangers beat on New Years Day?

20. Which former Rangers boss was in charge of the visitors that afternoon?

21. From which Club did Rangers sign defender Fitz Hall in January?

22. Which Chelsea striker scored the only goal of the game in the FA Cup third round tie at Stamford Bridge?

23. Which January signing scored eight goals in his first six appearances for the R's?

24. Against whom did Gavin Mahon score his first goal for Rangers?

25. How many clean sheets did Lee Camp keep last season?

26. Who scored twice in the R's 3-0 victory against Stoke City live on Sky Sports?

27. From whom did Rangers buy Republic of Ireland defender Damien Delaney?

28. Which teenage striker scored the R's goal in our 1-1 draw against Sheffield United in February?

29. Who was named QPR's Supporters' Player of the Year?

30. Which position did Rangers finish the 2007/08 Coca Cola Championship season?

THE SEASON

ANSWERS ON PAGE : 60

PARK

RENAULT F1

RENAULT F1 DAY

WHO SAID THAT?

"It was a nightmare watching the Rangers results on Soccer Saturday in the weeks leading up to the permanent transfer, because I just wanted to be playing football – and playing football for QPR."

1

"Bernie and I were delighted to receive a recommendation from the Board of QPR for our bid for the Club and we look forward to working alongside Gianni Paladini and his team.

We are fully aware of the history of QPR and the loyal fan base that it has; we are therefore totally committed to bringing future success back to the Club. Gianni, Bernie and I are all determined to see the Club return to the Premiership as soon as possible."

"It's very difficult to make the breakthrough at a Club like Arsenal, so when QPR made an offer I knew it was the right time to move on."

2

3

"The highs and lows of football never cease to amaze me. The bubble that we're in at the moment is unburstable. I look up to the Director's Box on a Saturday afternoon, be it home or away, and I see three of the wealthiest men in the world wearing QPR scarves - unbelievable!"

4

"For me, it will be an honour to work for Queens Park Rangers, a Club which is backed by Bernie Ecclestone and Flavio Briatore, two businessmen with an incredible track-record of success in sport and other fields."

6

"It's a really good feeling and I can't wait to show the fans that I am worthy of the number 10 shirt."

5

"I could have stayed at Preston for a few more years, and there were other clubs that were pursuing me, but QPR just felt like the right move."

"There is a great platform here - we have magnificent history; a great set of supporters; a superb stadium. Everything just seems to be right with QPR and we believe this is the perfect Club to do what we want to do - to take the Club back to where it belongs."

8

7

"I've no doubt that, player for player, this current QPR squad is better than the Watford squad that won promotion a few years ago."

9

"Asprilla did well in English football but I firmly believe my impact can be greater. That's not me being arrogant, it's just a show of the confidence I have in myself."

10

Key Quotes 07/08

ANSWERS ON PAGE : 61

OUR FUTURE

cargiant.co.uk
5,000 cars 5 mins from Loftus Rd

cargiant

OUR U18s

The BIG QPR Quiz

1

1. From which club did QPR sign defender Danny Shittu?

2. QPR secured their first division status in 1999 with a 6-0 victory over which London rivals?

3. In the 2007/2008 season how many goals did Akos Buzsaky score?

4. Who scooped Supporters' and Players' Player of the year in the 2006/2007 season?

5. QPR signed which Keeper from Derby County after having the shotstopper on loan during their 2003/2004 promotion campaign?

6. Who scooped Goal Of the Season in the 2006/2007 campaign?

7. AND against which club was this goal scored?

8. QPR beat which team in the second leg of the play-off final in 2002/2003 and what was the score?

9. Who wore the captains' armband in the Play Off Final versus Cardiff City?

10. QPR finished second to which club in the 2003/2004 season?

11. QPR signed fans' favourite Lee Cook from which club?

12. Who was leading scorer in the season 2006/2007?

13. How many club goals has Kevin Gallen scored for QPR...
    a) 77 b) 87 or c) 97?

14. QPR lost 5-1 at home to which Scottish giants in a 2007/2008 pre-season friendly?

15. QPR managers John Gregory and Luigi Di Canio both got off to 2-0 winning starts against which club at Loftus Road in consecutive seasons?

1. During the mid 70's QPR had no less than 6 players who gained full England caps - Name them.

2. QPR amalgamated in 1886 from which two teams?

3. When were these two clubs independently formed?

4. Who was the club mascot before Jude?

5. The 1967 League Cup Final attracted a competition record crowd at the time of 97,952 to Wembley - True or False?

6. QPR beat which club in the 1967 League Cup Final and by which score line?

7. QPR striker Don Givens gained 27 full international caps for which country?

8. QPR finished Division One runners up in which year and to which club?

9. In 1979 QPR thrashed which club 7-0 at Loftus Road?

10. Stan Bowles gained how many full England Caps?

11. QPR appeared in two Cup Finals in the 1980s, unfortunately losing both, one on a replay. Can you name the years, the Cup Competitions and the opponents?

12. Name the 2 Captains of the only ever QPR side to appear in an FA Cup Final and Replay.

13. Stan Bowles scored two hat tricks in a 2 leg UEFA Cup Tie against which opponent in 1976/77 Campaign?

14. Roy Wegerle was bought and sold by QPR for £1million - True or False?

15. Which QPR player scored a famous hatrick at Old Trafford versus Manchester United in the first game of 1992?

16. Which QPR Player won Goal of the Season (GOTS) for his efforts versus Barnsley in the 1996/97 season?

THE HISTORY

ANSWERS ON PAGE : 60

Ian Gillard
Left back (1968-82)
479 appearances / 11 goals

Phil Parkes
Goalkeeper (1970-79)
406 appearances / 0 goals

Paul Parker
Centre back (1987-91)
156 appearances / 1 goal

Alan McDonald
Centre back (1981-97)
476 appearances / 18 goals

Dave Clement
Right back (1967-79)
476 appearances / 27 goals

Gerry Francis
Midfield (1969-82)
347 appearances / 65 goals

Stan Bowles
Midfield (1972-79)
315 appearances / 96 goals

Dave Thomas
Left Midfield (1972-77)
220 appearances / 30 goals

Trevor Sinclair
Right Midfield (1993-98)
190 appearances / 28 goals

Rodney Marsh
Striker (1966-72)
242 appearances / 134 goals

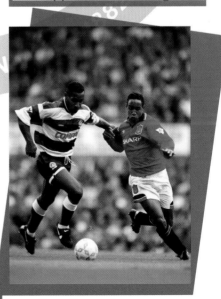

Les Ferdinand
Striker (1987-95)
170 appearances / 90 goals

ALBERTI

DE CARMINE

NEW SIGNINGS

LEDESMA

RAMAGE

Guess Who ?

1

2

5

3

4

6

WORD SEARCH...

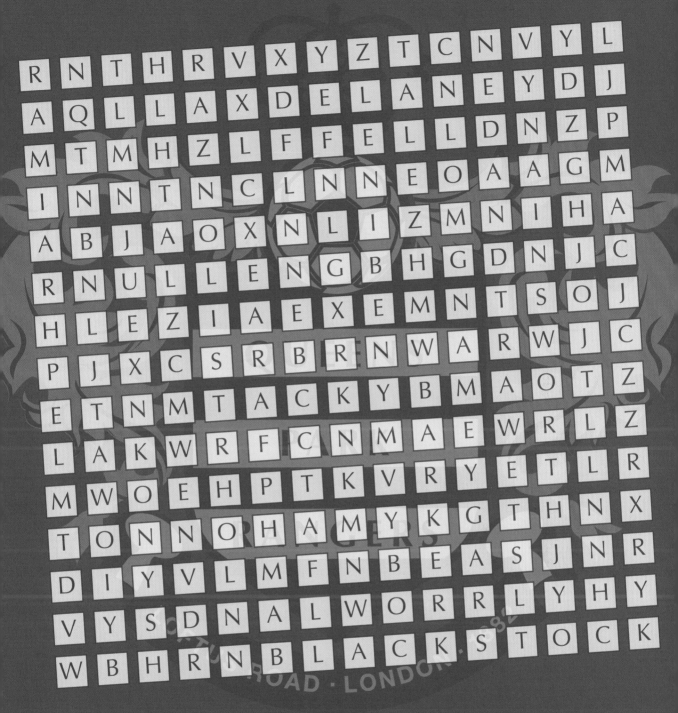

R	N	T	H	R	V	X	Y	Z	T	C	N	V	Y	L			
A	Q	L	L	A	X	D	E	L	A	N	E	Y	D	J			
M	T	M	H	Z	L	F	F	E	L	L	D	N	Z	P			
I	N	N	T	N	C	L	N	N	E	O	A	A	G	M			
A	B	J	A	O	X	N	L	I	Z	M	N	I	H	A			
R	N	U	L	L	E	N	G	B	H	G	D	N	J	C			
H	L	E	Z	I	A	E	X	E	M	N	T	S	O	J			
P	J	X	C	S	R	B	R	N	W	A	R	W	J	C			
E	T	N	M	T	A	C	K	Y	B	M	A	O	T	Z			
L	A	K	W	R	F	C	N	M	A	E	W	R	L	Z			
M	W	O	E	H	P	T	K	V	R	Y	E	T	L	R			
T	O	N	N	O	H	A	M	Y	K	G	T	H	N	X			
D	I	Y	V	L	M	F	N	B	E	A	S	J	N	R			
V	Y	S	D	N	A	L	W	O	R	R	L	Y	H	Y			
W	B	H	R	N	B	L	A	C	K	S	T	O	C	K			

Agyemang   Camp   Leigertwood

Ainsworth   Cole   Mahon

Balanta   Connolly   Mancienne

Barker   Delaney   Rehman

Blackstock   Ephraim   Rowlands

Buzsacky   Hall   Stewart

                                         Vine

ANSWERS ON PAGE : 61

CLUB
& COUNTRY

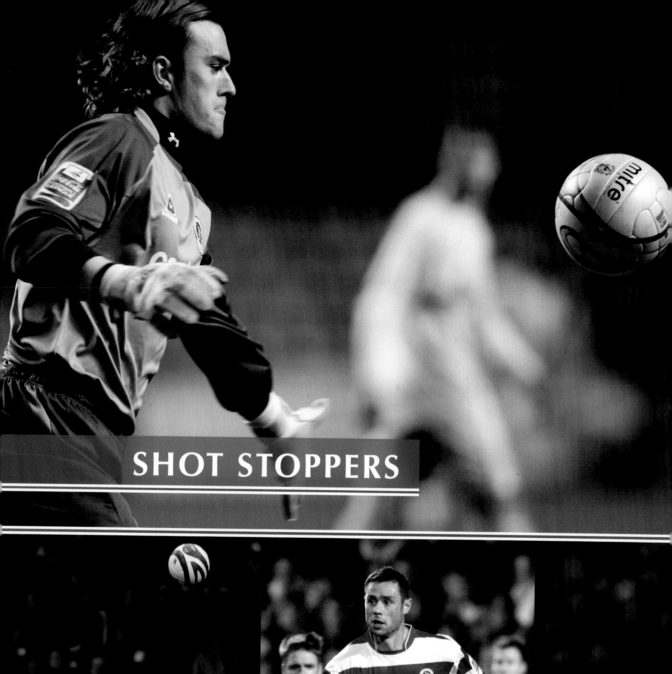

SHOT STOPPERS

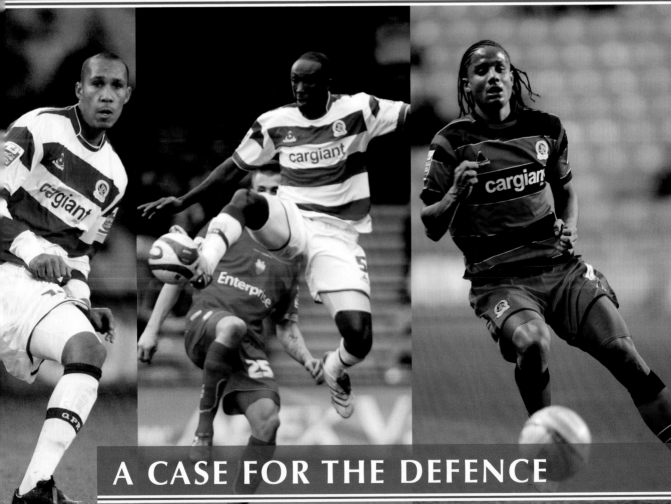

A CASE FOR THE DEFENCE

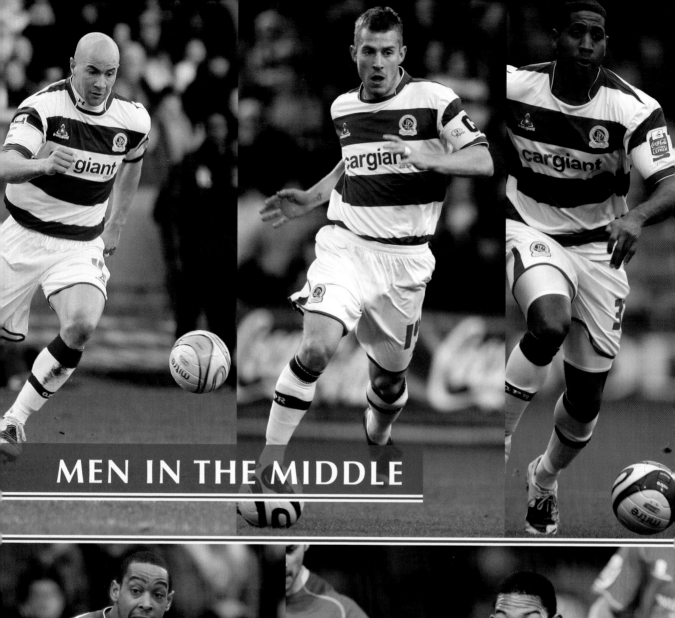

MEN IN THE MIDDLE

HOT SHOTS

57

GALLEN

Born in Chiswick in September 1979 Kevin Gallen had a phenomenal scoring rate as a youth player netting 126 goals in 2 seasons, which even surpassed the earlier record of legend Jimmy Greaves.

Gallen was a strong intelligent striker and was incredibly popular with the 'R's' faithful. The 'Kevin Gallen... Magic Hat' chant is one that has echoed from the W12 terracing on many occasions and the fact that the Gallen Family are QPR fans through and through endeared him even further to the Rangers Supporters.

Kevin Gallen made his QPR debut on the opening day of the 1994/95 season against Manchester United at Old Trafford and the Red Devils later tabled a 2 million pound bid for the No 10 as he struck up an impressive partnership with Les Ferdinand. Injuries plagued his career unfortunately, until his second spell at the club saw him play regularly under Ian Holloway and play a vital part in Rangers return to the Second Tier of English Football.

One of Kevin's proudest moments came when he was offered the Captain's armband by Holloway after being a driving force in Rangers promotion. The QPR No 10 scored 98 goals in 340 appearances for the Loftus Road Club making him the sixth highest goal scorer of all time for QPR.

BOWLES

Born in Manchester on Christmas Eve 1948, Stan Bowles signed for £112,000 from Carlisle United in September 1972 and went on to become arguably the finest and most popular player to have worn the QPR No. 10 shirt.

Stan was an unpredictable genius who won 5 full England Caps whilst at QPR. But his undoubted ability should have earned him more. Bowles netted 97 times in 315 League and Cup games for the Superhoops until the legendary Brian Clough took him to Nottingham Forest in December 1979 for £250,000. Although Stan was one of the great 'Mavericks' of the era he was also an incredible team player with great vision and energy and was surely one of the most unique talents this country has ever produced.

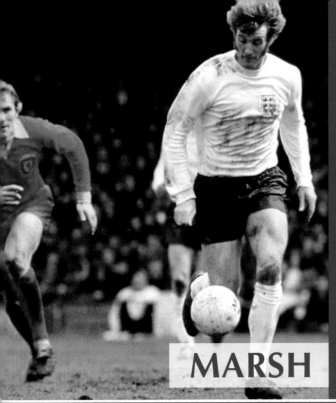

An enigma whose reputation precedes him and one of the most popular players to have ever worn the famous Blue and White Hoops and No. 10 Shirt of Queens Park Rangers.

Rodney was born in Hatfield, Hertfordshire on 11th October 1944 and he joined QPR from Fulham in March 1966 for £15,000.

This mercurial centre forward scored 134 goals in 242 League and Cup Games and not only netted an incredible 44 times in the 1966/67 season but also scored one of the greatest individual goals ever seen at Wembley.

The flamboyant No 10 was transferred to Manchester City in 1972 for £200,000. The cry of 'Rod-nee Rod-nee' would reverberate from Loftus Road terraces during his reign at the club.

MARSH

THE PERFECT 10

BUZSAKY

Following his move from fellow Championship side Plymouth Argyle, Akos Buzsaky - Young Hungarian Player of the Year in 2003 - was an immediate success at the club.

Buzsaky, blessed with outstanding natural ability, initially joined on-loan before making the deal permanent in January 2008. He scored six times in his first 13 appearances and ended the 2007/08 campaign with a total of 10 goals to his name.

Last season, the Hungarian international also scooped the Kiyan Prince Goal of the Season award following his quite sublime strike against Blackpool in March.

BIG Quiz (season) pg. 36-37

1. Dexter Blackstock
2. Leyton Orient
3. Rowan Vine
4. Gareth Ainsworth
5. Norwich City
6. Martin Rowlands
7. Mikele Leigertwood
8. Eight
9. Hogan Ephraim
10. Scott Sinclair
11. Dexter Blackstock
12. Akos Buzsaky
13. Luigi De Canio
14. Ray Jones
15. Wolverhampton Wanderers
16. Adam Bolder
17. 3-0
18. Danny Shittu
19. Leicester City
20. Ian Holloway
21. Wigan Athletic
22. Claudio Pizarro
23. Patrick Agyemang
24. Burnley
25. 14
26. Mikele Leigertwood
27. Hull City
28. Angelo Balanta
29. Martin Rowlands
30. 14th

QUEENS

PARK

RANGERS

1. Charlton Athletic
2. Crystal Palace
3. 10
4. Lee Cook
5. Lee Camp
6. Dexter Blackstock
7. Preston North End (PNE)
8. Oldham Athletic and QPR won 1-0
9. Steve Palmer
10. Plymouth Argyle
11. Watford
12. Dexter Blackstock
13. c) 97
14. Celtic
15. Hull City

1. Clement, Gillard, Parkes, Francis, Thomas, Bowles
2. St.Judes Institute and Christchurch Rangers
3. 1882
4. Arnie
5. True
6. West Bromich Albion (WBA) 3-2
7. Republic of Ireland/Eire
8. 1975/76 Liverpool
9. Burnley
10. Five
11. 1982 FA Cup Versus Tottenham Hotspur (Spurs) and 1986 Milk Cup Versus Oxford United
12. Glenn Roeder and Tony Curry
13. Brann Bergen
14. True
15. Dennis Bailey
16. Trevor Sinclair

BIG Quiz (history) pg. 44-45

60

Who Said That ? pg. 40-41

1. Hogan Ephraim
2. Flavio Briatore
3. Matthew Connolly
4. Gareth Ainsworth
5. Akos Buzsaky
6. Luigi De Canio
7. Patrick Agyemang
8. Amit Bhatia
9. Gavin Mahon
10. Angelo Balanta

Guess Who ? pg. 50

1. Mikele Leigertwood
2. Hogan Ephraim
3. Damion Stewart
4. Martin Rowlands
5. Angelo Balanta
6. Damien Delaney

Word Search pg. 51

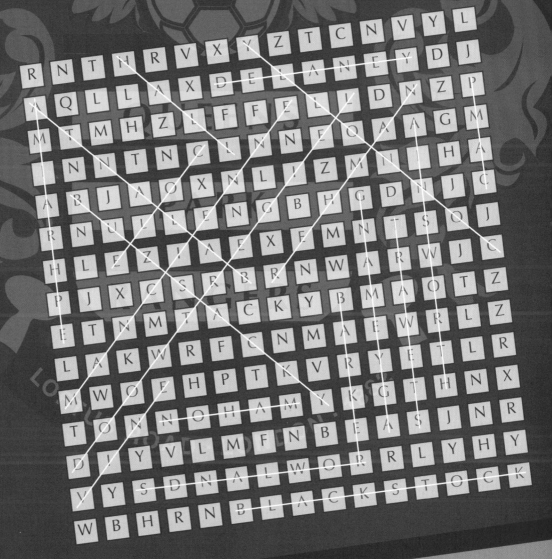

QUIZ ANSWERS

SIMPLY FAN-TASTIC!

QUEENS PA